St. Bernard

turtle

Koran angelfish

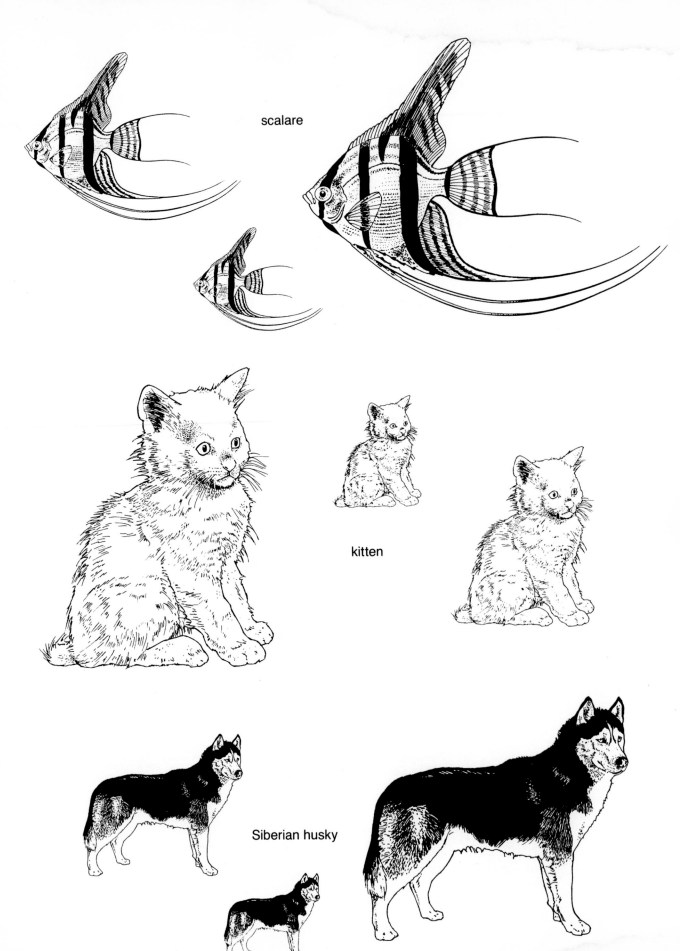

scalare

kitten

Siberian husky

2

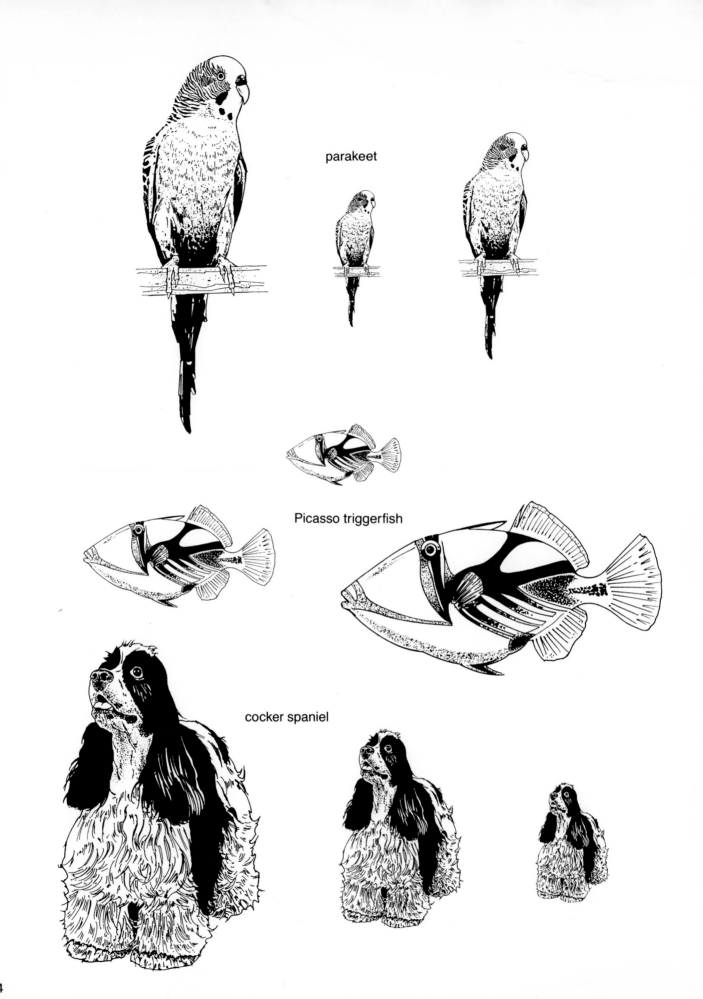

parakeet

Picasso triggerfish

cocker spaniel

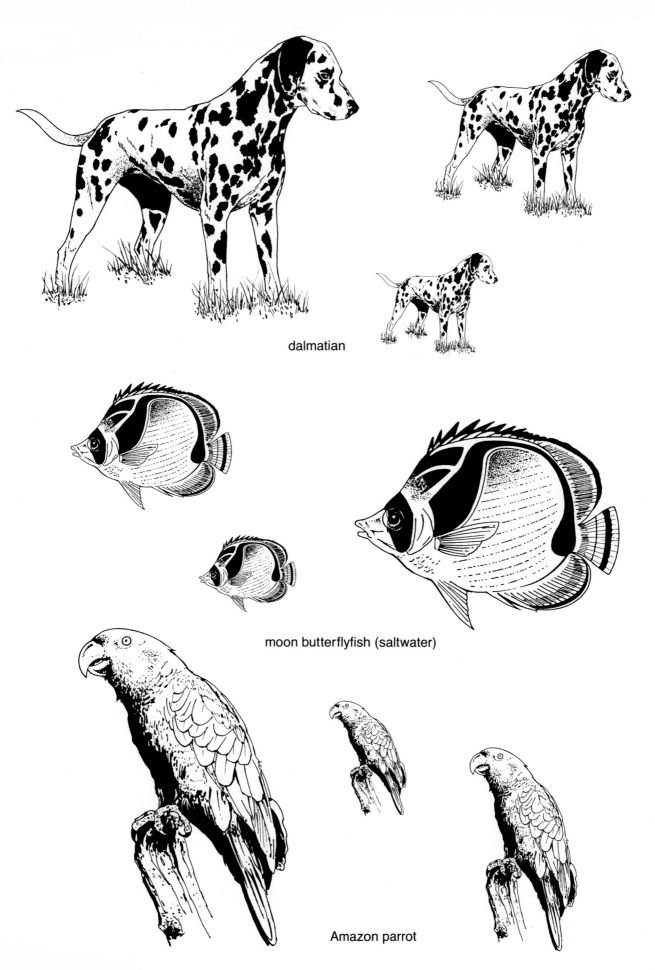

dalmatian

moon butterflyfish (saltwater)

Amazon parrot

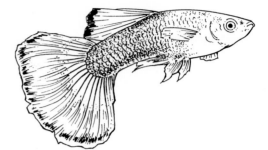

guppy

Burmese cat

weimaraner

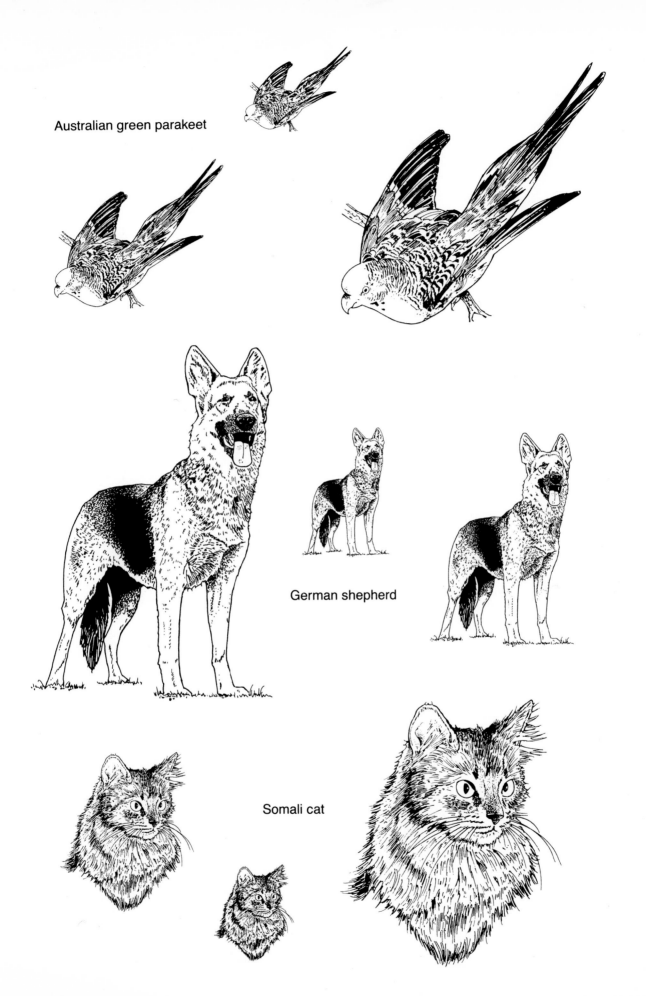

Australian green parakeet

German shepherd

Somali cat

homing pigeon

Angora cat

seahorse

8

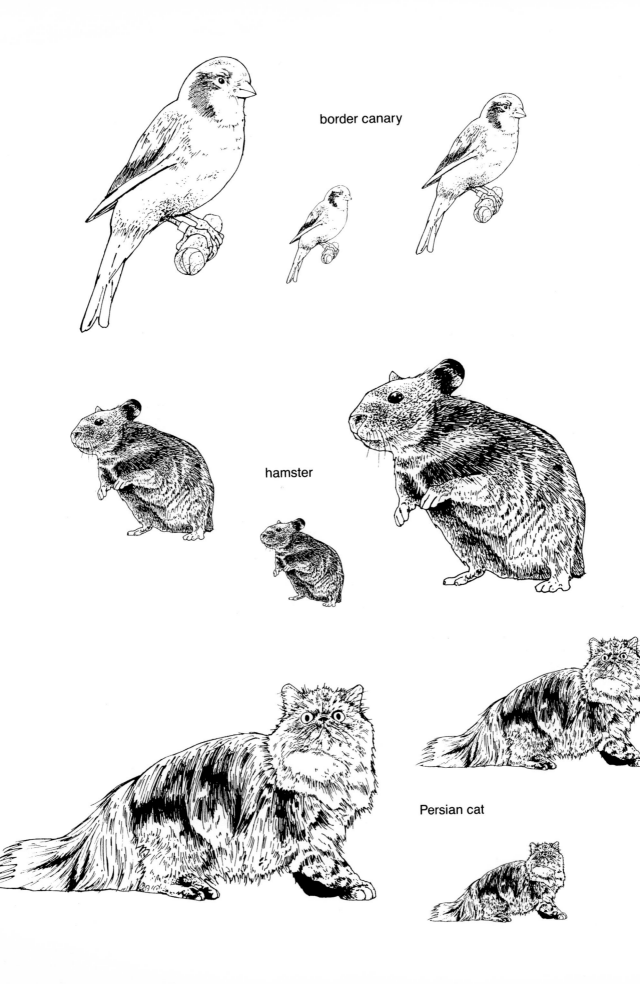

border canary

hamster

Persian cat

9

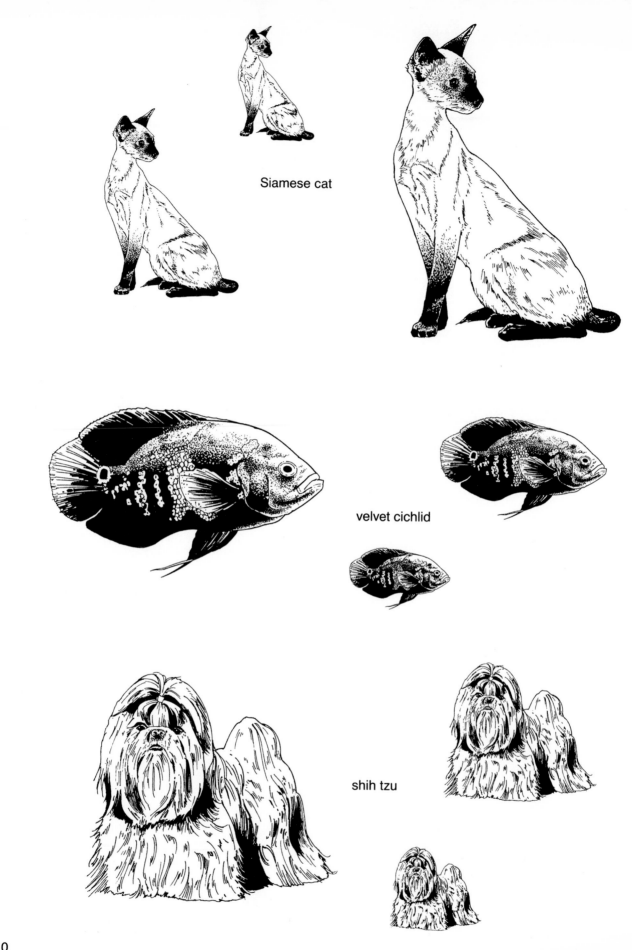

Siamese cat

velvet cichlid

shih tzu

 lined butterflyfish (saltwater)

boxer

iguana

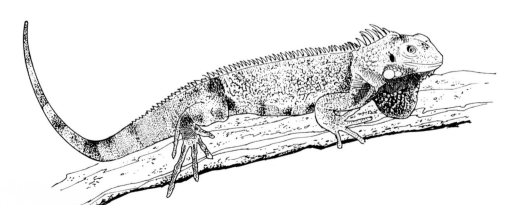

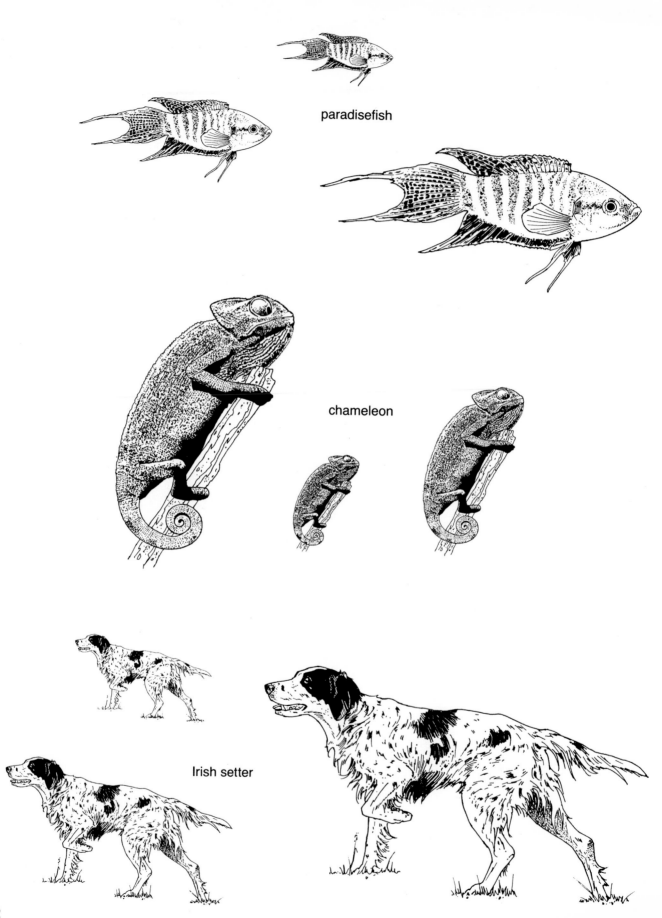

paradisefish

chameleon

Irish setter

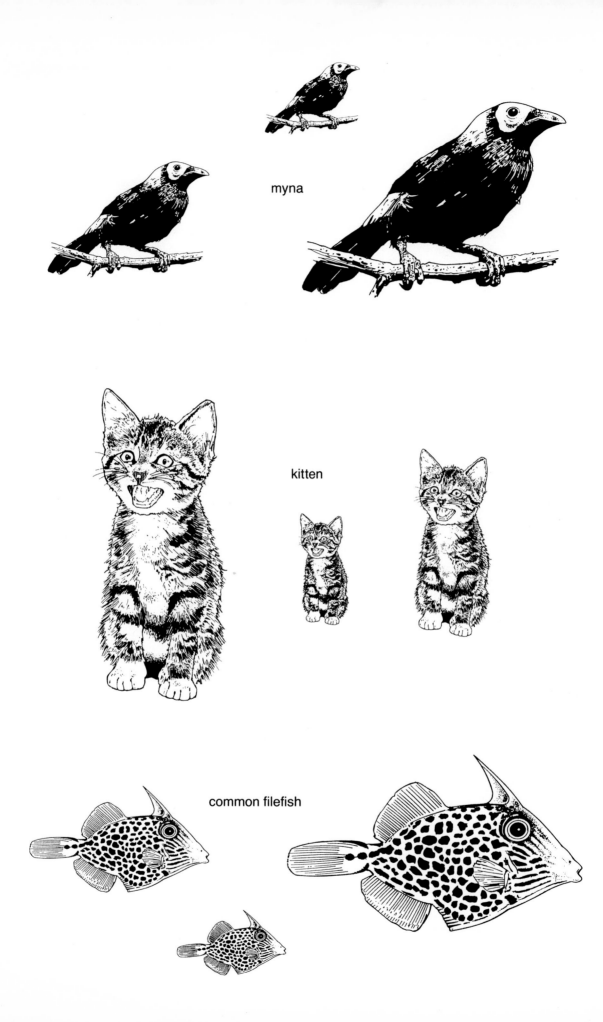

myna

kitten

common filefish

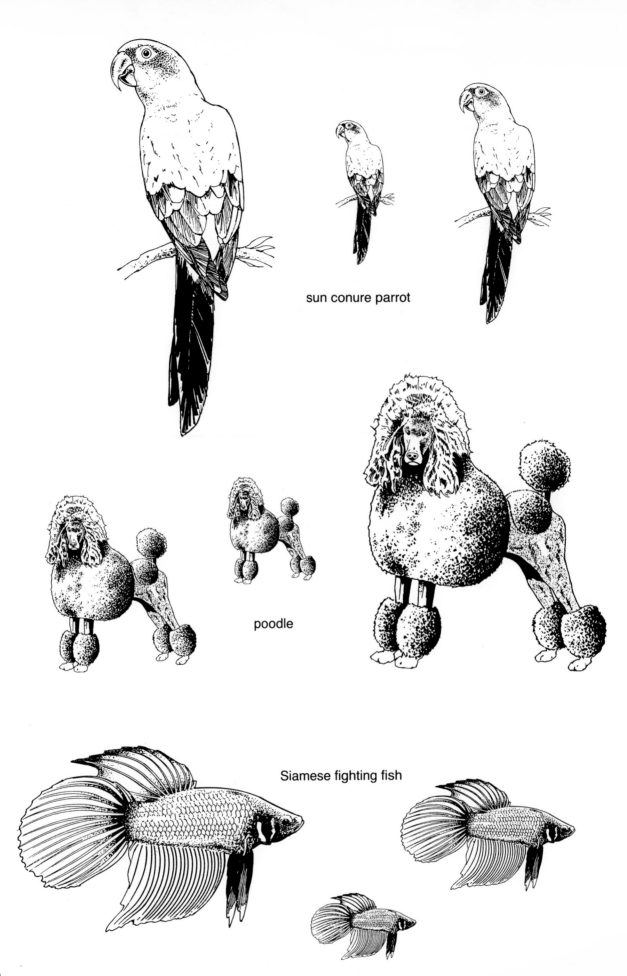

sun conure parrot

poodle

Siamese fighting fish

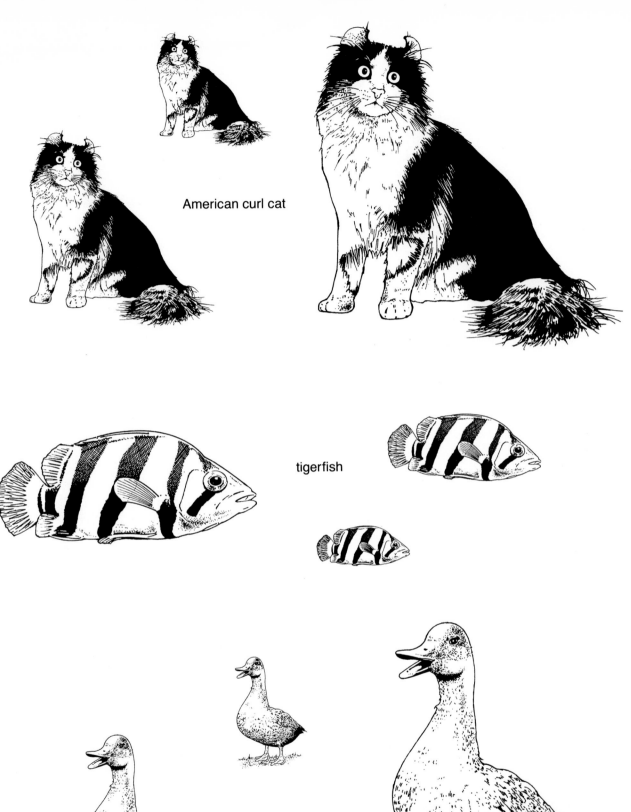

American curl cat

tigerfish

duck

sulphur-crested cockatoo

gecko

Maine coon cat

16

ferret

schnauzer

American mixed-breed cat

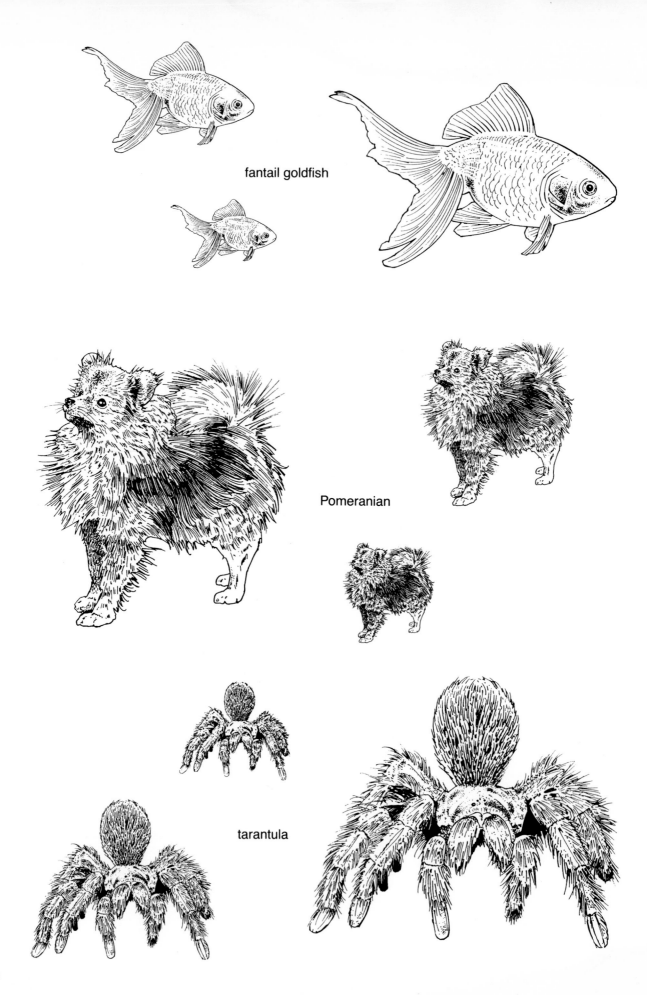

fantail goldfish

Pomeranian

tarantula

18

Russian blue cat

bearded collie

lovebirds

English sheepdog

canary

freshwater butterflyfish

bantam rooster

fox terrier

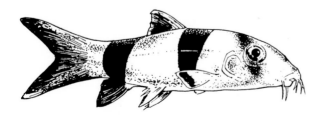

clown loach

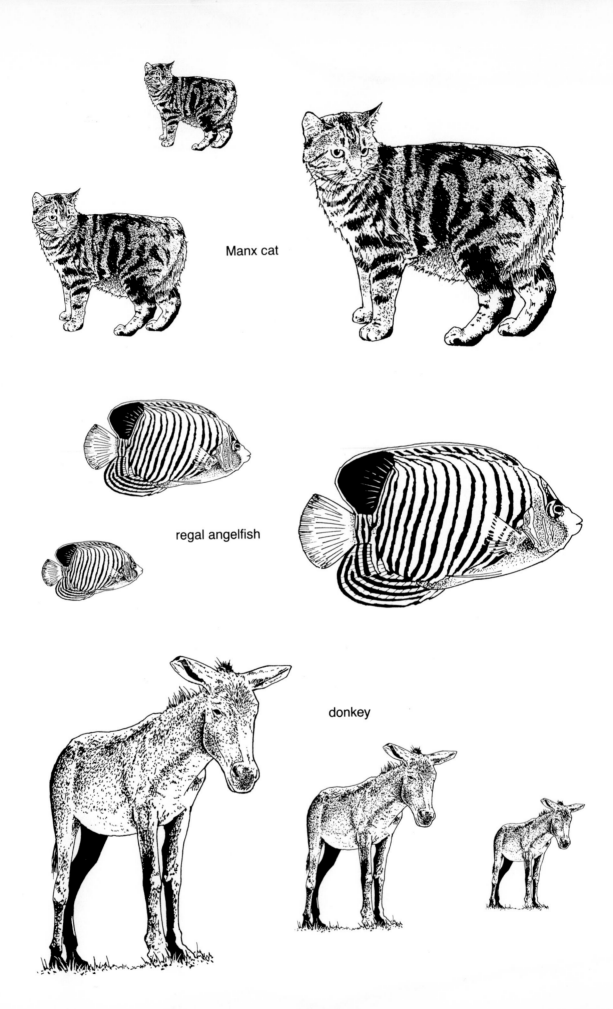

Manx cat

regal angelfish

donkey

22

bulldog

macaw

horned toad

Gloster corona canary

Great Dane

guinea pig

bichon frise

American shorthair tabby

pony

snowshoe cat

bullfrog

toy poodle

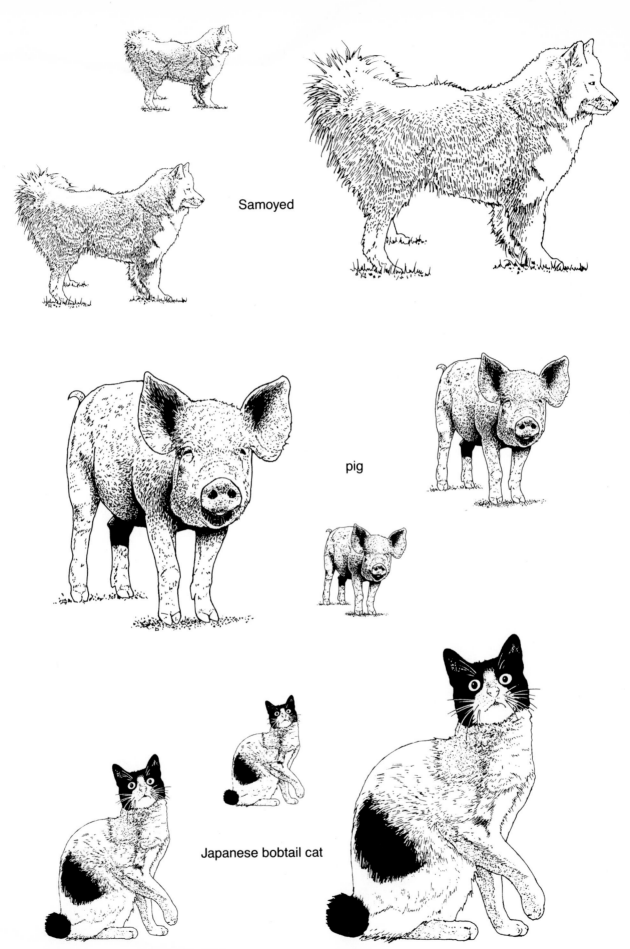

Samoyed

pig

Japanese bobtail cat

beagle

parakeet

miniature horse

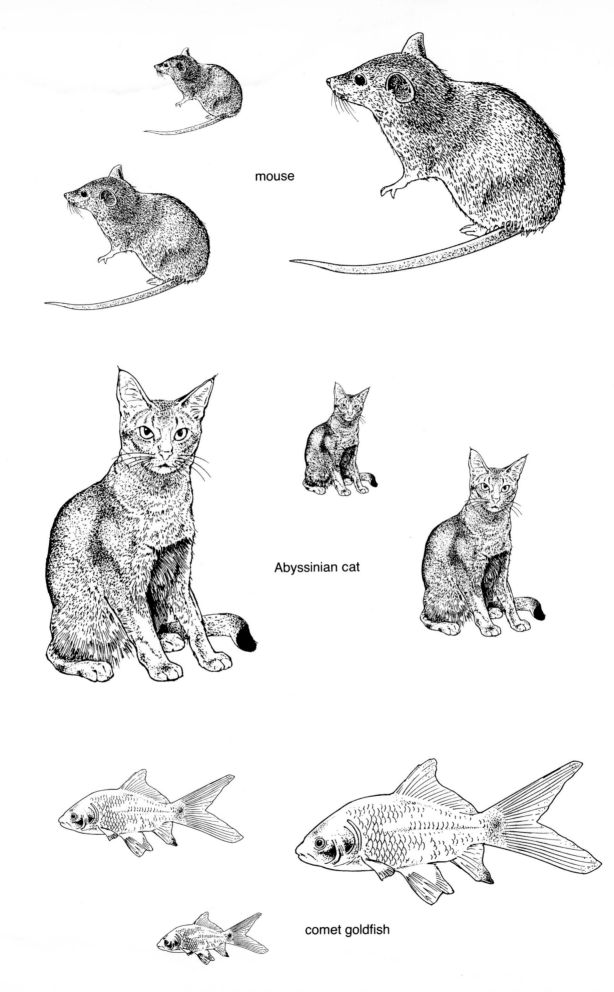

mouse

Abyssinian cat

comet goldfish

nightingale

flagtail catfish

Himalayan cat

Welsh corgi

cockatiel

gerbil

pale blue parakeet

golden retriever

basset hound

32